DUCT TAPE MANIA

Crafts, Activities, Facts, and Fun!

by Amanda Formaro

studio fun **BOOKS**

White Plains, New York • Montréal, Quebec • Bath, United Kingdom

Duct Tape Mania

Art Director: Karen Viola
Designer: Stephanie Weinberger
Editor: Elizabeth Bennett

Published by Studio Fun International, Inc.
44 South Broadway, White Plains, NY 10601 U.S.A. and
Studio Fun International Limited,
The Ice House, 124-126 Walcot Street, Bath UK BA1 5BG
All rights reserved.
Studio Fun Books is a trademark of Studio Fun International, Inc.,
a division of The Reader's Digest Association, Inc.
Printed in China.
Conforms to ASTM F963 and EN 71
10 9 8 7 6 5 4 3 2 1
HH2/03/14

Photo images by Amanda Formaro with the exception of the following:

Title page: ©Gerald Bernard/Shutterstock.com; Page 3: ©oksana2010/Shutterstock.com; Page 4: ©Andrey_Kuzmin/Shutterstock.com;
©Vjom/Shutterstock.com; Page 6: ©leedsn/Shutterstock.com; ©Olga Kovalenko/Shutterstock.com; Page 9: ©OneSmallSquare/Shutterstock.com;
Page 15: ©Tristan3D/Shutterstock.com; Page 19: ©jackhollingsworth.com/Shutterstock.com; Page 23: ©Nattika/Shutterstock.com; Page 29:
©Gerald Bernard/Shutterstock.com; Page 33: ©PeterVrabel/Shutterstock.com; Page 34: ©nito/Shutterstock.com; Picsfive/Shutterstock.com;
Page 37: ©BlueOrange Studio/Shutterstock.com; Page 38: ©Sabelnikov/Shutterstock.com; Page 39: ©donatas1205/Shutterstock.com;
Page 42: ©Juriah Mosin/Shutterstock.com; Page 46: ©Boris15/Shutterstock.com; Page 46: locker (modified) ©Zimiri/Shutterstock.com;
Page 47: ©WBB/Shutterstock.com; ©EM Arts/Shutterstock.com; Page 49: ©photovs/Shutterstock.com; Page 50: bike (modified)
©MNStudio/Shutterstock.com; Page 51: ©Valeriy Lebedev/Shutterstock.com (top left); ©HomeArt/Shutterstock.com (top right);
©MaZiKab/Shutterstock.com (bottom left); ©Alexander Mak/Shutterstock.com (bottom right); Page 52: ©ILYA AKINSHIN/Shutterstock.com;
©prochasson frederic/Shutterstock.com; Page 53: ©viewgene/Shutterstock.com; Page 57: ©David Davis/Shutterstock.com;
Page 62: ©Pavel L Photo and Video/Shutterstock.com; Page 63: ©stockphoto mania/Shutterstock.com; Page 67: ©David Philips/Shutterstock.com.

Page backgrounds and graphics: ©donatas1205, ©J.D.S., ©pun photo, ©Radiocat, ©Roman Samokhin, ©Roman Sigaev, ©Ronald Sumners/Shutterstock.com

Most of the projects in this book were made using Duck® brand duct tape. Duck® brand tape is a trademark of Shurtech Brands, LLC.
This book is in no way associated with or endorsed by Shurtech Brands, LLC.

Library of Congress Data has been applied for.

A Note to the Reader:
When engaging in any activities suggested in this
publication, children should always be under adult
supervision. Any references in this publication to
any products or services do not constitute or imply
an endorsement or recommendation.

Contents

How do you start a book about duct tape?
With an Intro-**DUCT**-tion!

If you've never played around with duct tape before, we're warning you, it can be habit forming! In fact, you are likely to get stuck on this awesome new craze! Once you've tried making one or two things with duct tape and realize just how easy it is, you'll be hooked.

That's why we're here! We'll show you all the amazing ways you can turn an ordinary roll of duct tape into a cool craft project, a fun game you can play, or even pretty accessories you can wear.

We'll also show you some nifty tricks, like how to keep your cutting tools from getting all sticky and how you can use duct tape to help you in everyday situations. Sure, there are plenty of projects inside these pages, but be sure to watch for little tips throughout the book that will help you get the most out of your rolls of duct tape.

Are you ready to get started? Grab a roll and go!

No skills? No sweat! Look for this symbol for our simplest crafts.

Crafting Rock Star? Look for this symbol for our harder crafts.

Sticky Tips

- ✔ Scissors are great for cutting small pieces of tape and for cutting curved shapes.

- ✔ Regular scissors are fine, but you may want to get a pair of non-stick scissors from your craft store.

- ✔ To clean the tacky stuff that sticks to your scissor blades, try wiping them with a bit of mineral oil or petroleum jelly.

- ✔ Use a ruler (one with a cork back is great) to cut straight lines.

- ✔ A craft knife is great for cutting long strips. Use a self-healing cutting mat to protect your work surface. The mats are also great because they have all kinds of guidelines for measuring and keeping things straight.

- ✔ **Remember—craft knives are sharp,** so you should have a parent help you when you use one.

- ✔ It's easy to lift a piece of tape that is stuck to the craft mat by using the tip of your knife blade to lift up a corner of the tape.

Just the Basics

Standard duct tape width is 2"

MAKE A BAND

1. Cut a piece of tape to the length you want.
2. Place the tape, sticky-side-up, on your surface.
3. Fold one long edge up about ⅓ of the way toward the middle.
4. Fold the other long edge over to the edge of the fold and smooth it out.

MAKE A STRING

1. Cut a piece of tape to the length you want.
2. Place the tape, sticky-side-up, on your work surface.
3. Fold about ⅛ inch along one long edge over onto itself. You can put a ruler ⅛ inch in from the edge of the tape to fold up again.
4. Fold that fold over again.
5. Continue folding until you have one long skinny strip—a string!

MAKE A BRAID

1. Tape three strings down on your work surface. They should be very close to each other.
2. Cross the right strip over the middle strip so it is now the middle strip.
3. Cross the left strip over the new middle strip.
4. Repeat steps 2 and 3 until you have braided all the strips.
5. Braid as tightly as you can.

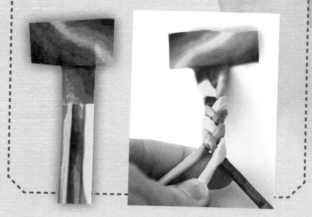

MAKE A SINGLE-SIDED SHEET

1. Roll out a piece of tape to the length you want. Stick it down on your work surface.
2. Stick a second strip of tape down, overlapping the first strip about ¼ inch.
3. Keep adding strips until you have the size sheet you want.
4. Lift the whole sheet off your work surface. Trim the edges if necessary.

MAKE A DOUBLE-SIDED STRIP

1. Cut two pieces of tape to the length you want.
2. Place one piece sticky-side-up on your work surface.
3. Stick the other piece of tape on top of the first piece, lining up all the edges.
4. Smooth out any bubbles.

MAKE A DOUBLE-SIDED SHEET

1. Make two single-sided sheets. You should make each sheet a little bigger than the size you want.
2. Stick the two sheets together.
3. Trim to make it the right size.

Friendship Bracelet

Make pretty braided bracelets in a variety of colors and patterns, all in a matter of minutes! Use your favorite colors or make school spirit bracelets by braiding in your team's colors.

1 Measure and cut three 12-inch strips of tape. For solid-colored braids, use just one color. Use 1, 2, or 3 colors for varied looks.

3 Fold the strip into a string (see page 6). Repeat for the other two strips.

2 Place a strip of tape, sticky-side-up, on the work surface.

4 Line up all three strips together and secure one end with a piece of tape. Tape that to the work surface so that you can snugly braid all three strips together. (See page 7 for braiding tips.) When finished braiding, secure the end with a piece of tape.

5 Place braided tape around your wrist. You will need enough room to be able to slip the bracelet over your hand to take it off.

6 Trim as needed.

7 Finally, secure both ends together with a piece of tape.

FUN FACT!

Believe it or not, there is a duct tape capital of the world. Springfield, Missouri, claims to have sold more duct tape per capita (that means per person) than any other place in the world!

Fish Tail Bracelet

Sometimes called fish bone braiding, this type of braid uses two main strands and ends up looking like the rows of ribs in a fish. For a wider bracelet, simply use more duct tape strings!

1 Make six 10-inch-long duct tape strings (see page 6).

2 Gather all six strings together and attach them to the work surface with a piece of tape.

3 Separate the strings so that you have three on one side and three on the other.

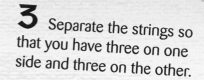

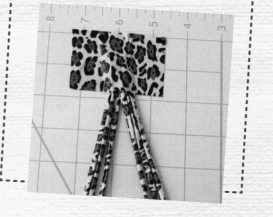

4 Take the string that is farthest to the left and cross it over the top of the other strings on the left, resting it with the three strings on the right.

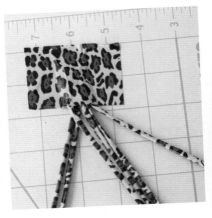

5 Take the string that is farthest to the right and cross it over the top of the other strings on the right, resting it with the three strings on the left.

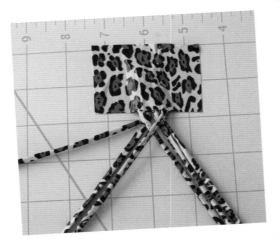

6 Repeat steps 4 and 5 until you reach the end of the strings.

7 Measure your finished braid and trim the length with a craft knife to fit your wrist.

8 Gather one end of the strings together and stick it to a one-inch-wide piece of tape. Leave about ¼ inch of tape above the end of the bracelet. Place one of the magnet buttons at the end of the strings.

9 Roll the tape around the strings and magnet and press the remaining exposed sticky tape down onto the magnet.

10 Repeat steps 8 and 9 on the other end of the bracelet.

11 To wear your bracelet, place it around your wrist and connect the magnet ends together.

TACKY TIP:
Be sure you line up the magnets so that when they touch, they attract. One side attracts and the other side repels!

Chain Bracelet

If you've ever made a bubble gum wrapper chain bracelet, this piece of jewelry is right up your alley. If you've never made one, grab your duct tape and craft knife—that's all you'll need to make this fun project!

1 Measure and cut six strips of tape, each nine inches long. If using six colors, cut one strip from each color.

2 Use the craft knife to cut each of those strips in half, creating a total of twelve 4½-inch strips.

3 Use the craft knife to cut those 12 pieces in half lengthwise, for a total of 24 strips.

4 Fold each strip over onto itself lengthwise, leaving a small amount of sticky side showing. Fold that sticky piece down so that there are no exposed sides.

5 Fold one thin strip in half lengthwise and crease in the center. Open it back up and fold both ends toward the center crease. Then, fold at the center crease, enclosing the folded ends inside. This is one link.

7 Repeat step 6 over and over again, to create the entire chain bracelet.

6 You will need to create a second link (see step 5) to join to the link you just created, starting the chain. To join these two links together, insert the folded ends of one link into the looped ends of the other link.

8 When ready to close, be sure the bracelet fits your wrist (remove any excess links if necessary) so that you will be able to slip it on and off.

9 Carefully open the folds of the first link in the chain and insert the last link into the folds. Secure with small strips of tape that match that link color.

TACKY TIP:
As an alternative, you can use small Velcro® dots as a closure for the bracelet.

STICKY situation

Out of wrapping paper?
Press duct tape directly on the gift box. Make designs or cover in stripes and then add decorative touches by cutting shapes, letters, and motifs from tape to attach to the "wrapped" surface.

Beads, Beads, Beads!

It's easy to make pretty beads using duct tape! Use them to make bracelets, key chains, backpack tags, necklaces, and earrings. These beads would also be fun to string onto yarn during the holidays for a festive garland!

Straw Beads

1 Measure and cut a strip of duct tape approximately the same length as a drinking straw and place it on your work surface, sticky-side-up.

2 Place the straw along the long edge of the tape.

3 Roll the straw up inside the tape.

4 Trim the ends of the straw to make the tape and straw ends even.

What You Need:

- ✓ Drinking straws
- ✓ Duct tape
- ✓ Scissors
- ✓ Ruler
- ✓ Craft knife
- ✓ Cutting mat

5 Cover more straws with different patterns of duct tape if you want.

6 Cut the straw into sections to create the beads.

Rolled Beads

1 Measure and cut a 10-inch-long strip of duct tape.

2 Cut that strip in half lengthwise.

3 Use a ruler to cut each strip in half on the diagonal, creating four long triangles.

4 Stick the wide end of the triangle to a drinking straw and slowly roll the tape around the straw. To add a second bead to the same straw, leave a little space in between each one and repeat the process. Or cut the straw into smaller pieces before you begin to roll.

5 Trim the ends of each bead so there's no straw showing.

TACKY TIP:
Add store-bought beads for fancier designs!

FUN FACT!

Duct tape has become so popular that the amount sold every year could stretch as far as the moon (maybe even a little farther)!

Duct Tape Roll Bracelet

When you finish off a roll of tape, don't toss out that cardboard roll. Instead, make fun bangles and cuff bracelets to wear to school or hanging out with your friends!

What You Need:
- ✓ Empty tape roll
- ✓ Duct tape in your favorite colors and patterns
- ✓ Craft knife or scissors
- ✓ Cutting mat

Bangles

1 Cover the cardboard roll in duct tape.

2 Use other colors or patterns to decorate the bangle any way you like!

Cuff Bracelets

1 Use a craft knife or scissors to cut out a 3-inch section of the empty cardboard roll.

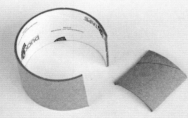

2 Cover the cardboard cuff with duct tape.

3 Use other colors of duct tape to decorate the cuff.

4 For a fun decoration, create a braid from three colors of duct tape. Cut a strip of tape the same length as the cuff and roll it up, sticky side out. Stick it to the cuff then stick the braid to the sticky tape. Trim ends of braid and secure them to the ends of the cuff, using the same color tape as the base of the cuff bracelet.

TACKY TIP: You can gently bend in the sides of the cuff bracelet to make it smaller.

TACKY TIP TWO: With the help of an adult, you can try cutting an empty roll into smaller, narrower rings to make a bunch of bangles from one roll!

Hair Bows

From tiny tot to all grown up, girls just love hair bling! Make these pretty bows in whatever size you like and use with hair ties, barrettes, and even as lapel pins.

What You Need:

✓ Duct tape in your favorite colors and patterns

✓ Barrette, bobby pin, hair tie, or lapel pin

✓ Scissors

✓ Ruler

1 For small bows, measure and cut a 13-inch strip of tape and a 2-inch strip of tape. For larger bows, start with a 20-inch strip of tape.

2 Fold the small piece of tape in thirds to make a band (see page 6). Set aside.

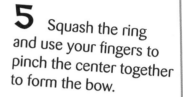

3 Fold the long piece of tape lengthwise, sticky side to sticky side, leaving about ½ inch of sticky side visible.

4 Bring the ends of the tape together to form a ring, using the sticky end to close the ring.

5 Squash the ring and use your fingers to pinch the center together to form the bow.

6 Wrap the small piece of tape around the center of the bow and secure with another small piece of tape.

7 To add a barrette or bobby pin, use a piece of tape to attach the hair clip to the bow, leaving the other half of the barrette or bobby pin free to clip into your hair.

17

Belt

Bling out your wardrobe with your favorite duct tape colors and patterns! It's easy to do by making several different belts to go with your outfits. Belt buckles are available at craft supply stores.

What You Need:
- ✓ Duct tape
- ✓ Scissors
- ✓ Craft knife
- ✓ Cutting mat
- ✓ Belt buckle

1 Measure and cut enough duct tape to go around your waist, plus add about six inches, or simply use one of your existing belts as a cheat sheet!

2 Make a band from your length of tape (see page 6).

4 Use your craft knife to make a hole in the center of the crease. Poke the buckle's prong through the hole.

3 Fold over one inch from an end and crease.

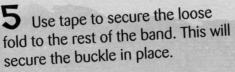

5 Use tape to secure the loose fold to the rest of the band. This will secure the buckle in place.

6 Use scissors to round the corners of the opposite end of the band.

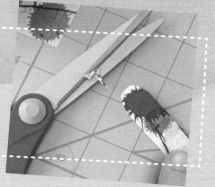

7 Use your craft knife (or a small hole punch) to make five holes, about one inch apart, starting about four inches from the curved end.

8 Cut a one-inch-wide strip of tape and fold into a band to create the loop.

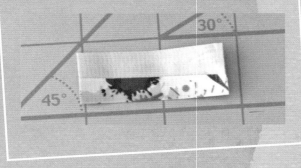

9 Wrap the band around the belt, about three inches from the buckle, and secure to the back of the belt with tape.

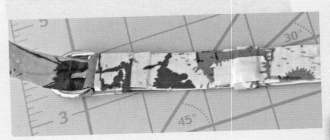

Wallet

One of the projects that started the duct tape craze is the duct tape wallet. While wallets can be made with photo ID slots, zippers, and tri-folds, starting with a basic bi-fold design is the way to go!

1 Using patterned tape, make a double-sided sheet (see page 7) that measures 8 x 6".

2 Measure and cut an 8-inch strip then cut it in half lengthwise to create two 8-inch-long narrow strips. Stick one of the narrow strips along one of the 8-inch sides of the double-sided sheet, folding over to the other side. This will hide any cut edges. Repeat this process for the other 8-inch side of the sheet.

3 To make the card pockets, create a 15-inch-long double-sided strip (see page 7) with patterned tape.

4 Measure and cut two 15-inch-long narrow strips like you did for the 8-inch strips in step 2.

5 Set one narrow strip aside. Stick the second narrow strip to the bottom of the double-sided strip, allowing half overlap. Do not fold over; leave the sticky side exposed for now.

6 Measure and cut a 15-inch-long narrow strip of solid colored tape.

7 Place double-sided strip with the excess strip, sticky-side-down, on the cutting mat. Stick one of the narrow solid colored strips to the top of the double-sided strip, overlapping by ¼ inch.

8 Turn over the double-sided strip, exposing the sticky sides of both the top and bottom strips. Fold over the top strip (solid colored), leaving the bottom exposed. Turn entire double-sided strip over, and with sticky-side-down, cut into four equal 3¾-inch pieces to make the card pockets.

9 Fold your 8 x 6" sheet in half, creating an 8 x 3" wallet body.

CONTINUED →

21

10 Hold the wallet body with your hand and line up one of the pockets, sticky-side-down, along the left edge of the wallet body, about ½ inch from the top. Press the sticky side of the pocket to the wallet body.

11 Place the second pocket below the first one, lined up along the left side, about ½ inch below the top of the first pocket. Press the sticky side down and turn the wallet body over. There should be some exposed excess; press it to the back of the wallet.

12 Repeat steps 10 and 11 for the pockets on the right side.

13 From your remaining narrow patterned strip, cut two 3-inch-long sections. Use these pieces to cover the left and right sides of the wallet body, folding over from front to back.

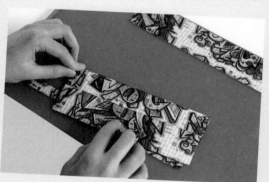

14 Cut a 3½-inch piece from the remaining narrow patterned strip. Lining it up along the bottom of the wallet, run the strip up the center, covering the pocket edges, and fold it over inside the wallet.

Zippered Pencil Pouch

No, you don't have to use a sewing machine to add a zipper to this pencil pouch. In fact, when you see just how easy these are to make, you'll ask yourself why you didn't think of this before!

What You Need:

✓ Duct tape
✓ Gallon-sized plastic zipper bag
✓ Craft knife
✓ Cutting mat
✓ Scissors

1 Lay storage bag on the cutting mat and cut off four inches from the bottom of the bag.

2 Tape down the corners of the bag to hold it in place on the cutting mat.

3 Starting just below the bag's zipper enclosure, cover the bag with strips of duct tape, overlapping the edges a bit.

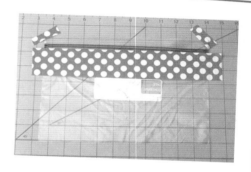

4 When bag is completely covered, pick it up and turn it over.

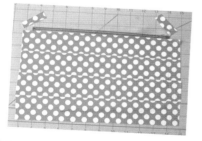

5 Fold the excess tape over onto the back of the bag.

6 Cover the other side of the bag with duct tape, again overlapping the sides a bit.

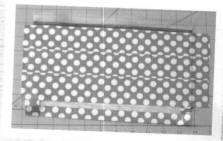

7 Turn bag over and fold over excess tape.

8 Cut strips from a different color or pattern of tape to cover the edges and add a decorative border.

TACKY TIP: Start your own business! Make these in your school colors and sell them to your classmates at the beginning of the school year.

Water Bottle Carrier

Tired of lugging that water bottle around in your hand? Make your own water bottle carrier, complete with handle, and you'll never be wondering where you left your bottle.

1 Make a double-sided sheet (see page 7) about one inch larger on all sides than the diameter of your water bottle.

2 Place your water bottle in the center of the square and use a craft knife to cut a slit that runs from each corner to the edge of the water bottle.

3 Remove the water bottle. Lift one corner of the sheet. Cross the two sides of that cut corner over each other to create a rounded corner. Stick together with a small piece of tape.

4 Repeat step 3 for each corner until you have a small cup.

5 Lay your water bottle on its side on your cutting mat.

6 Based on of the size of your water bottle, create another double-sided sheet the height of your water bottle, and long enough to wrap around the bottle with a couple of inches extra. Trim any exposed sticky edges from the sheet.

7 Line the inside of your duct tape cup with pieces of tape so that the sticky side is partially exposed, facing outward.

8 With your large double-sided sheet laying on the mat, place the cup with sticky tape exposed along its bottom edge.

9 Roll the sheet around the cup, pressing the sticky tape in place as you go. Tape up the open sides of the carrier body.

10 Make a band (see page 7) for the carrier handle. The length is up to you, ours is 18-inches long.

11 Tape the ends of the band to the inside of the top of the carrier.

12 If you would like to add a border or stripes, do that now. You can cover the seam (where the cup meets the sheet) if you want and/or put a stripe up at the top.

WARNING! It is likely that you will be asked to make one of these for everyone on your team!

25

Tablet Case

Whether it's for your phone, MP3 player, e-reader, or tablet, a customized case is fun to make and is a great way to carry your device.

What You Need:

✔ Duct tape in one solid color and one pattern

✔ Scissors

✔ Your device(s)

1 Because the size of devices varies, you will need your device handy to determine the size of the duct tape sheet you will need to make.

2 Create a double-sided sheet (see page 7) that is wide enough for your device plus two more inches and 2½ times the length of your device.

3 One side of the sheet should be the solid-color tape. The other side of the sheet should be the pattern.

4 Place your device on the solid colored side of the sheet. Fold the bottom of the sheet up over your device. Adjust until there is only about ½ inch of your device showing.

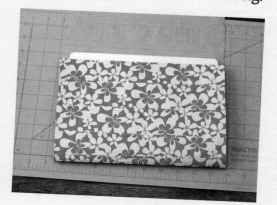

5 Trim the sides of the sheet, leaving about ½ inch extra on either side of your device.

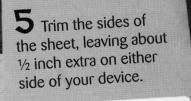

6 Create a border around the yellow side of the sheet using patterned tape.

7 Fold up the cover again and close the sides of the sheet with patterned tape. Slide your device inside.

8 Make a band (see page 6) out of solid-colored tape long enough to wrap completely around your case. This will be used to close your case.

10 Fold flap down and insert into band.

9 Wrap the band around the tablet cover, positioning it so the flap can be tucked into it. Connect the ends of the band on the back and secure them to the back using patterned tape.

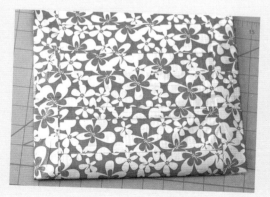

TACKY TIP:
Now that you know the basics, go to town! Make a smaller case for your cell phone. Make a bigger case to cover a laptop. Make cases for your friends!

27

Purse

No matter what size purse you want, use this easy design to create the perfect bag just for you! Choose your favorite colors and patterns to make the design your own!

1 Lay denim on your work surface, wrong side facing up.

2 Place a strip of your patterned tape along the 11-inch side of the denim. Note: If you prefer vertical stripes, run the tape in the other direction, along the 18-inch side.

3 Place a solid-colored (e.g., yellow) strip of tape just overlapping the edge of the patterned tape. Continue to alternate strips of tape in a pattern as you move across the denim.

4 Repeat until all the denim is covered.

5 Turn the taped fabric sheet over and trim all edges of excess tape.

6 Fold the sheet in half lengthwise so that the taped side is showing and the denim is inside. Use a strip of duct tape to close the left and right side, leaving the top open. Trim off the ends of the tape.

7 Use patterned tape to line the opening of your bag by taping all the way around the top.

8 To make the bottom of the bag flat so your purse can stand up, use your finger to push the corners of the bag inside the bag. This will create a couple of flaps inside the bottom of your bag. Secure them down with patterned tape.

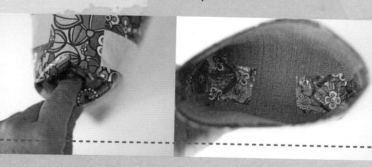

9 Run patterned tape across the bottom and up the sides inside the bag.

10 Measure and cut an 11-inch piece of patterned tape. Fold it in half, sticking it to itself so that it now measures 5½ inches long. This will be the closure strap. Set aside.

CONTINUED →

FUN FACT!

Avon, Ohio, really knows how to celebrate our favorite sticky material. Every year they have a Duct Tape Festival that features a parade of floats made out of… duct tape! The festival also has crafts, games, concerts, and more!

11 Cut two rectangles of patterned tape approximately 3 x 2" and place them sticky side up.

12 Place one magnet in the center of each of the pieces of tape.

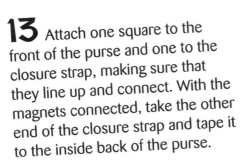

13 Attach one square to the front of the purse and one to the closure strap, making sure that they line up and connect. With the magnets connected, take the other end of the closure strap and tape it to the inside back of the purse.

14 To make the handle, braid three 36-inch strips of tape together (see page 7 for braiding instructions).

15 Secure the end with a piece of tape. Use patterned tape to attach the handle inside the sides of the purse.

Light Switch Cover

A great way to add some personal flair to your room is by dressing up your light switch covers. All you need is your favorite duct tape (and your parent's permission!).

1 Have your parent shut the power off, then help you remove the light switch cover from the wall.

2 Cover the whole front with duct tape.

3 Trim the edges of the tape close to the edge of the cover. Too much excess could cause problems with the switch plate fitting properly.

4 Cut a hole for the light switch lever.

BEWARE! Covering light switch covers with duct tape can be habit forming!

What You Need:

✓ Light switch cover
✓ Duct tape
✓ Craft knife

5 Be sure to poke holes for the screws before getting a parent to help you put the light switch cover back on the wall.

31

What You Need:

✓ Duct tape in one or more colors or patterns
✓ Pen or pencil
✓ Craft knife
✓ Ruler
✓ Cutting mat

Flowers

Duct tape flowers are kind of like potato chips: You can't stop at just one! Soon there won't be a pen or pencil in the house that's not topped with one of these lovely blooms!

1 Measure and cut 30 pieces of duct tape measuring 2½ inches each.

2 Take one piece of tape and fold the right corner down so it almost meets the other side. Note: You will leave about ½ inch of sticky tape showing at the bottom.

3 Fold the opposite side up to create a triangle. Repeat for all 30 pieces.

4 Place the eraser end of the pencil about ¼ inch below the point of a petal, with the sticky side touching the pencil.

PIN & PLEAT FABRICS & UPHOL

5 Wrap the sticky side of the tape around the pencil to secure the first petal.

6 Line up a second petal directly across from the first petal and stick it to the pencil.

7 Line up a third petal in between the first and second, and stick it to the pencil.

8 Line up the fourth petal directly across from the third and stick to the pencil. Continue attaching petals around the pencil, placing the points of new petals in between points of existing petals.

TACKY TIP:
You can add leaves by creating petals from green tape and attaching them to the bottom of the finished flower.

FUN FACT!

DUCT TAPE OR DUCK TAPE?
Actually both names are correct. The sticky stuff was originally used by the army to keep dampness out of ammunition cases. Its waterproof quality earned it the name "duck" tape. After World War II, construction workers found that the tape worked well to connect heating and air-conditioning ducts. Hence the name change from duck to duct! Today, Duck® is a brand of duct tape.

😎 Vase

Whether it's a recycled chip canister or a thrift store vase, duct tape is a fun way to add color to a room. Perfect gifts for holidays such as Valentine's Day and Mother's Day as well!

1 Cover cylinder with duct tape.

2 Decorate the vase using strips of a contrasting tape to make stripes, or cut designs from a patterned tape like we did.

STICKY situation

Pants too long?
Turn your pants inside out. Fold over to the desired length. Secure with duct tape!

Clothes Hangers

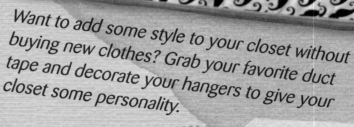

Want to add some style to your closet without buying new clothes? Grab your favorite duct tape and decorate your hangers to give your closet some personality.

1 Lay the hanger on a cutting mat and cover one side with strips of tape.

2 Turn the hanger over and cover the other side.

3 Trim the edges with scissors or a craft knife.

4 Cut a contrasting-color strip of tape into four long strips. Use strips to cover the edges of the hanger, folding them over so they cover both sides.

5 Use another strip of the same contrasting tape to wrap around the neck and hook of the hanger.

IT'S A WRAP!
Try covering a plastic hanger by simply cutting strips of tape and wrapping them all around the edges of the hanger.

Banner

Brighten up any wall in your room with this fun and colorful banner made from—what else?—duct tape!

What You Need:

✔ Duct tape in two colors or patterns
✔ Scissors
✔ Baker's twine (available at craft store)
✔ Embroidery needle with large eye

1 Make a double-sided sheet (see page 7) that measures 18-inches-long and 4-inches-wide.

2 Cut your sheet into 11 triangles, each three inches at the wide end.

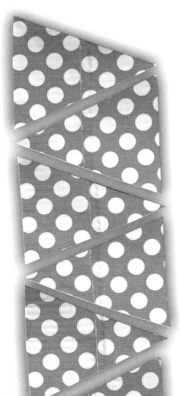

3 Repeat steps 1 and 2 with your alternating color/pattern.

4 Decorate the triangles with additional pieces of duct tape if you want.

5 Thread your needle with baker's twine and poke it through one corner wide end of a triangle. Bring the thread back through the other corner. Connect all of the triangles together using this method.

6 You can slide the triangles along the string to place them as close together or as far apart as you like.

What You Need:

- ✓ Lamp shade
- ✓ Duct tape
- ✓ Craft knife
- ✓ Cutting mat

Lamp Shade

Turn an ordinary lamp into something stylish using, you guessed it, duct tape! You choose the design that fits your personality. Whether it's flowers, polka dots, stripes, or a variety of other patterns, it's easy to do and makes a fun addition to your homework desk or nightstand. But be prepared—your mom may ask you to make one for the living room!

1 Measure and cut one or more 15-inch strips of duct tape.

2 Use a craft knife to cut designs.

3 Lift designs with the tip of your craft knife and press onto the outside of your lamp shade.

Stylin' Frames

Here's a great way to bring new style to a boring old frame. If you don't have a frame to cover, pick one up at a thrift store, garage sale, or even the dollar store, then give it a makeover with duct tape.

What You Need:
- ✓ Picture frame
- ✓ Duct tape

STICKY situation

Need a bandage?
Fold a tissue or paper towel to cover the wound and cover this with duct tape. It may not be attractive, but it works in a jam.

1 Be sure the picture frames are clean to ensure that tape will stick.

2 Remove backing and glass from frame.

3 Completely cover frame with tape.

4 Replace glass.

5 Insert photo and securing backing.

Desk Organizers

Decorate your homework desk and get organized in style with your favorite colors and patterns. All you need are some boxes and containers from the recycle bin to get started!

What You Need:
- ✓ Duct tape in at least one solid color and one pattern
- ✓ Recycled items such as boxes, cans, plastic jars, ribbon spools, etc.

1 Cover recycled items using duct tape.

2 Decorate and embellish using another color or pattern of duct tape.

3 Place items on desk and fill with pens, pencils, paper clips, and note pads.

4 Voila!

39

Book Jacket

What You Need:
- ✓ Duct tape color(s) and/or pattern(s) of your choice
- ✓ Brown paper grocery bag
- ✓ Scissors
- ✓ Book to be covered

No need for boring paper bag book jackets when you can jazz them up with duct tape. Add a little personality by using your favorite colors and patterns!

1 Cut off the bottom of the brown paper grocery bag.

2 Cut the bag open by cutting from the top of the bag to the bottom along one of the sides. You should have a long rectangle when finished.

3 Lay book in the center of the bag. Fold and crease the top and bottom of the bag down so that the height of the bag is equal to the height of your book.

4 Open the book and fold the left side of the paper around the cover of the book. Repeat this on the other side of the book as well.

5 To make sure your book jacket fits snugly, insert the actual book's cover into the opening of your paper bag jacket. Repeat on the other side.

6 Remove the jacket from the book.

7 Cover the outside of the paper bag with strips of duct tape, making sure you do not tape the opening shut.

8 Once covered in duct tape, put the jacket back on the book. Decorate with additional duct tape to create stripes or other designs.

Personalized Pencils (and Pens)!

Here's a quick way to decorate your pencils (and pens)! Choose your favorite duct tape colors or patterns to make them your own.

What You Need:
- ✓ Duct tape
- ✓ Pencils and/or pens
- ✓ Scissors

STICKY situation

Is your folder torn?
Duct tape is perfect for repairing a school folder. Run tape down the length of the spine or cut shorter pieces to run across the bottom.

1 Cut strips of duct tape the same length or shorter than your pencils.

2 Wrap tape around your pencil's (or pen's) body. You can make stripes, or cover the whole pencil.

TACKY TIP: This works great with mechanical pencils, too!

Pencil Toppers

Dress up the ends of your pencils lickety-split with these fringed designs. Super easy and ready in a flash. Perfect for back to school!

1 Measure and cut a 4-inch strip of duct tape.

2 Fold the tape over onto itself, leaving about ¼ inch of sticky tape exposed.

3 Use a craft knife or scissors to cut slits in the folded side of the tape, creating a fringe affect.

4 Lay the top of your pencil onto the end of your fringed strip with the sticky side touching the pencil.

5 Roll the pencil up in the fringed tape, pressing the sticky side to the pencil as you wrap.

43

Clipboard

Add some pizzazz to a boring clipboard by decorating it with duct tape! Add a coordinating pencil and you have the perfect gift!

1 Cover the front of the clipboard with strips of duct tape. The strips should be longer than the width of the clipboard. Don't fold the edges over just yet.

2 Turn the clipboard over and cover the back with tape. These strips should be slightly smaller than the size of the clipboard. Fold the overlapping edges of tape from the front of the clipboard onto the back.

3 Decorate your clipboard with contrasting tape. Stripes work great, or use a craft knife to cut shapes from patterned tape to attach to your board.

Clothespin Note Clips

😎

Clothespins are pretty handy. You can use them to organize a bunch of hair ties or baseball cards, keep a chip bag closed, even mark your place in a book! Make a bunch of these duct tape-covered clothespins and we bet you'll find even more uses!

What You Need:

✓ Duct tape (one or two colors or patterns)
✓ Craft knife
✓ Cutting mat
✓ Wooden clothespins

Library books due TOMORROW!

1 Lay a piece of duct tape a little longer than your clothespin, sticky-side-up on the cutting mat.

2 Place the flat side of your clothespin onto the sticky side of the tape and press down so it sticks well.

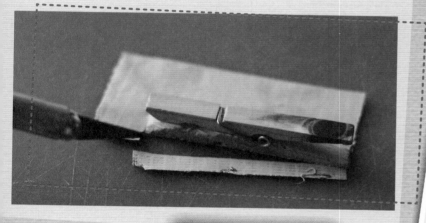

3 Use a craft knife to trim the excess tape around the edges of the clothespin.

4 Using another piece of tape, cover the other side of the clothespin.

STICKY situation

Kissed a frog?
Believe it or not, duct tape can be used to heal a wart. Check with a parent, then cut a small piece of duct tape to cover the wart. Leave on for about a week. Take off the tape. Wash the area. Repeat for another week or two until the wart is gone.

Locker Style

It's the beginning of the school year and you want your locker to stand out. Well, grab a roll (or two) of duct tape and let the stylin' begin!

✓ Hang a banner (see page 36).

✓ Cover a mirror.

✓ Frame a friend (see page 38).

✓ Add flair to a wipe-off memo board.

✓ Design a notebook cover.

✓ Make your clipboard an original (see page 44).

✓ Organize your pencils (see page 39).

Math Test Tomorrow!

Bookmarks

Don't lose your place! Keep track of where you are in your favorite books with these easy-to-make bookmarks!

What You Need:

✓ Duct tape (one or two colors or patterns)

✓ Craft knife or scissors

✓ Cutting mat

✓ Yarn or embroidery thread

✓ Paper clips

1 Measure and cut a 7-inch strip of duct tape.

2 Measure and cut four 11-inch pieces of yarn or embroidery thread.

3 Gather the pieces of yarn together and place them in the center of the strip of tape so that one inch hangs off of one end and three inches hang off the other end.

4 Fold the tape into thirds, over the yarn, sandwiching it in the middle.

5 Use a small piece of tape to attach a paper clip to the back of the bookmark (at the end with the longer pieces of yarn).

6 Never lose your place again!

STICKY situation

Chips get stale?
To keep a half-finished bag of chips fresh, fold up the top and seal it tight with a piece of duct tape.

CHIPS

Braided Jump Rope

If you can braid, you can make your own customized jump rope in your favorite colors. Your friends will all want one, so be prepared to show them how to make their own!

What You Need:

✔ Duct tape in up to four colors/patterns
✔ Scissors or craft knife
✔ 2 chairs
✔ Measuring tape

1 Place two chairs 12 feet apart from each other.

2 Stick a piece of tape to the back of one of the chairs and stretch it out to the other chair, sticking it in place. Repeat this step for the other two strips.

3 Without removing the tape from the chairs, fold one of the strips of tape in half, sticking it to itself. Get as close to the end of the strip as you can without removing it from the chair.

4 Repeat this step for the other two strips.

5 Reposition the tape on one of the chairs so that all three strips are close together.

6 Remove the strips from the second chair and fold the ends of the tape as you did in step 3.

7 Beginning at the end of the strips that are still attached to the chair, braid the three strips together tightly until the entire 12 feet of tape has been braided. See page 7 for help with braiding.

8 Measure and cut two 6-inch strips of tape for the handles. Wrap the tape around the last six inches of the braid on one end. Repeat with the second strip for the other handle.

TACKY TIP: We made an 8-foot jump rope, which is the right length for someone who is between 4'10" and 5'3". If you are taller, you may want to add another foot of braid, which will take 1½ feet of additional tape. Remember, braiding shortens the amount of tape you started with!

49

Spiffy Sports

What You Need:

✓ Duct tape (lots of colors and patterns)

✓ Bicycle

Deco-Bike

1 Cut a length of duct tape.

2 Wrap it around your bike frame.

It's as simple as that!

TACKY TIP: Want to get fancy? Make streamers to tape to your handlebar grips (see Pom-Poms on page 56 for instructions).

More Sticky Sports Tips

If you have ever tried tricks on your skateboard, you know how quickly you wear down your shoes. Well, you can breathe some extra life into those sneakers if you add a layer or two of duct tape to the areas that scrape along the board. And while you are at it, why not decorate the bottom of your skateboard with some colorful strips of tape?

Street hockey sticks really take a beating. So why not wrap the bottom of your stick with duct tape. You can replace the tape as often as you need to and make your stick last longer!

Soccer or hockey player? No need to worry about loose shin guards if you have a roll of duct tape handy. Put on your socks first, then your shin guards. Now wrap duct tape around your shin guard to keep it tight to your leg.

STICKY situation

Trip over your laces?
Have your ever tripped over an untied lace during an important game? That won't happen if you wrap duct tape around your shoes or cleats after you tie them.

Scrap Ball

Once you start creating with duct tape, it's kind of hard to stop! All that cutting, snipping, and trimming leaves you with plenty of little sticky scrap pieces that can get in the way of your project. Every duct tape creator should have a scrap ball. You can start one by just wadding up a piece of duct tape in your hands. Continue sticking your scraps to it and before you know it, it will have grown to epic proportions! Well, maybe not epic, but it'll be big!

STICKY situation

Clothes covered with lint?
Wrap your hand with a length of duct tape, sticky-side-out. Then roll the sticky tape against your clothing in a rocking motion until every last speck has been picked up.

Duct tape balls are great for playing catch, football, hopscotch, dodgeball— you name it!

Indoor Hopscotch

What You Need:

- ✓ Duct tape in three colors/patterns
- ✓ Craft knife
- ✓ Cutting mat
- ✓ ¼ cup dried beans or rice
- ✓ Sandwich bag

Sure, you can draw a hopscotch board on your driveway with chalk, but what about days when it's rainy or the temperatures are just not fit for playing outdoors? You can set up your very own hopscotch game using a roll of duct tape! You can even make a quick beanbag to toss instead of the customary rock.

1 Make a double-sided sheet (see page 7) measuring 4 x 4".

2 Make a second double-sided sheet in a different color or pattern, also measuring 4 x 4".

3 Measure and cut two 4-inch strips of the third color duct tape. Cut those strips in half lengthwise so that you have four narrow 4-inch-long strips.

4 Use the strips of tape to attach three sides of the two squares together, leaving one side open.

5 Place beans inside sandwich bag and use an extra scrap of tape to keep the bag closed tight around the beans.

6 Insert the bag of beans into the opening and use the last narrow strip to close the beans inside.

7 Use duct tape to create a hopscotch grid on your floor or carpet.

8 Hop away!

Football Game

Known as paper football, this game is usually played with a folded-up piece of paper and either lost or tossed out later. This durable football mat can be brought out again and again for hours of fun, seeing who can kick the highest goals and score the most points. For footballs, use duct tape in favorite team colors or brown to keep it traditional.

What You Need:

✓ Duct tape: green, white and brown (or team colors)

✓ Craft knife

✓ Cutting mat

✓ Ruler

✓ Scissors

✓ 2 sheets of paper

First the Field

1 Make a green double-sided sheet (see page 7) the same size of your cutting mat.

2 Use scissors to trim off any exposed sticky tape from all sides.

3 Measure and cut one strip of white tape the full length of your cutting mat. Use a craft knife to cut that strip lengthwise into four narrow strips.

4 Use one of these white strips to edge each side of your green sheet. Trim any excess. Your green sheet should now have a white border.

5 Measure and cut two mores strips of white tape, the same width as your cutting mat. Then cut each strip into eight skinny long strips.

6 Find the center of your green sheet and stick one of the skinny strips across the center to make the "50 yard line."

54

7 Measure 1½ inches from the right side of the green sheet. Stick a skinny strip across the sheet at this mark to create the "end zone."

8 Repeat step 7 for the opposite end zone area.

9 Add three more skinny strips between the 50-yard line and the end zone on the left. Repeat this for the right side as well.

10 From the remaining skinny strips, add "yard markers" by cutting ½-inch pieces, sticking them between each of the long skinny strips on the green sheet.

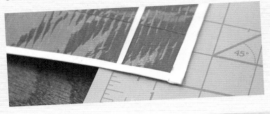

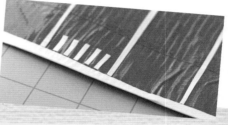

TACKY TIP: Because the skinny strips used for the yard markers and for the footballs are so small, it's easiest to lift the corner off the cutting mat with the tip of your craft knife, then hold that piece of tape in place with your finger and lift the strip off the mat. Use your craft knife to place it onto the surface and press in place with your finger.

KICK OFF!

Now the Footballs

1 To make a football, fold a sheet of paper in half lengthwise and in half again.

2 Fold one corner up to create a triangle. Take that triangle and fold upward again. Continue folding upward until there's no room left to fold.

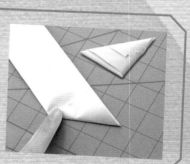

3 Secure any excess paper around the triangle with a small piece of tape.

4 Cover the footballs in brown duct tape, or use tape in your favorite team colors. Cut skinny strips of white tape (or team colors) to add football stitches.

What You Need:

✓ Duct tape in two colors or patterns

✓ Scissors

✓ Craft knife

✓ Cutting mat

✓ Ruler

Pom-Poms

Rah Rah Sis Boom Bah! Show your team spirit by making this set of colorful pom-poms to shake at the big game! Better yet, plan a group craft party with friends to make some for everyone.

1 Make six 18-inch double-sided strips (see page 7) in two different colors or patterns for a total of 12 strips.

2 You will use three strips of each color for each pom-pom. Keep the strips for each pom-pom separated.

3 Cut a double-sided strip into narrow strips measuring approximately ¼ inch each. One double-sided strip will yield eight or nine narrow strips.

4 Cut the long narrow strips in half, creating 9-inch-long narrow strips.

5 Choose one color tape to use for the pom-pom handles. From that cut a 12-inch strip and lay it sticky-side-up on the work surface.

6 Lay the tops of all the narrow strips for one pom-pom onto the 12-inch handle strip.

7 Measure another 12-inch strip in the same color and tape it over the top of the narrow strips, sandwiching them inside.

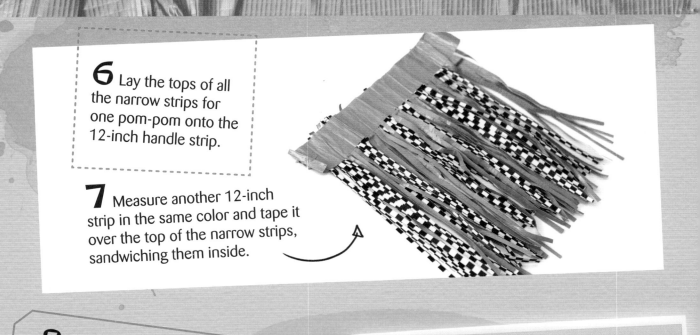

8 Starting at one end of the 12-inch strip, roll up the strip, creating the handle and encasing the narrow strips as you roll.

9 Cut a strip of handle color tape and cover the top of the handle to enclose everything.

Gimme a **T**
Gimme a **A**
Gimme a **P**
Gimme a **E**

What's that spell?

Well, you know how it goes...

10 Repeat steps 6 through 9 for the second pom-pom.

Road and Town

What could be more fun than a town made of duct tape? Make it as small or as big as you like—create a sprawling town or simple road for toy cars. Buildings are made from recycled boxes and everything else is duct tape!

What You Need:

- ✓ Recycled boxes (crackers, light bulbs, shoe boxes, etc)
- ✓ Gray and yellow duct tape (road)
- ✓ Various colors of duct tape (buildings)
- ✓ Craft knife
- ✓ Ruler
- ✓ Cutting mat

Beep! Beep!

1 Measure and cut a strip of gray duct tape the full length of your cutting mat.

2 Measure and cut a second piece of gray tape the same length. Stick it along side the first piece, overlapping by about ¼ inch, creating one long double-wide strip. Repeat this step until you have created a road that is your desired length.

58

3 Measure and cut a strip of yellow tape the full length of your cutting mat.

4 Using your craft knife cut the yellow tape into a long thin strip, about an ⅛ inch wide.

5 Cut that strip into ¼-inch-long pieces.

6 Lift the corner of one of the pieces with the tip of your craft knife to lift the tape off of the mat. Use the craft knife to carry the yellow tape over to the gray tape strip and stick it to the center of the strip.

7 Repeat steps 6 and 7 until all of your roads have the yellow stripe dividers.

8 Cover empty recycled boxes with duct tape. Cut squares from yellow tape and add to the boxes as windows.

Extra Stuff

Wind Spinner

Create a beautiful wind spinner for your yard or garden with a recycled plastic bottle and colorful duct tape. These spinners are really fun to watch and will help keep the crows out of your garden as well.

What You Need:

✓ Recycled plastic bottle
✓ Duct tape (one pattern, one solid)
✓ Craft knife
✓ Cutting mat
✓ Small paper clip
✓ Snap swivel (available at any store where you can buy fishing tackle)
✓ Fishing line

1 Wash and dry the bottle, removing any labels.

2 Cover the middle section of the bottle with solid duct tape.

3 Cut narrow strips of patterned duct tape to add stripes over the solid duct tape.

4 Use your craft knife to cut vertical slits in the bottle from the top of the tape to the bottom of the tape. The slits should be about ¾ inch apart.

5 Stand the bottle up on a table and press down on the top of the bottle. This will collapse the center, pushing the cut sections of the bottle out.

6 Hold bottle in place and crease each section in its center.

7 Angle the sections by making folds at the top and bottom of each strip. This allows the wind to catch them and make it spin. At the top of each strip twist to the right. At the bottom of each strip twist to the left.

8 Using your craft knife, poke a small hole in the top of the bottle cap.

9 Unfold and stretch the paper clip out and thread it through the looped end of the swivel.

10 Twist the paper clip together then insert it into the hole in the top of the bottle cap.

11 Bend the ends of the paper clip so that it can't come back out the hole. Then screw the top back on the bottle.

12 Tie a piece of fishing line to the top end of the swivel and hang your wind spinner in your yard. Let the spinning begin!

Duct Tape Magic

What You Need:

✓ Duct tape*

✓ A dark room

*This works with some brands of duct tape better than others. Experiment with a few brands to see what works best for you.

Want to wow your friends? Grab a roll of duct tape and turn out the lights to demonstrate how tape makes sparks! Want to really impress them? Tell them this phenomenon is called **triboluminescence**. It even sounds like magic!

1 Make a double-sided strip (see page 7), leaving one end open so that there's an inch or two not stuck together.

2 Hold the tape at the open ends with both hands.

3 Turn off the lights.

4 Pull the tape apart from the open ends.

5 As the tape separates, a line of blue light that appears to glow or looks like a spark, will appear.

Holiday Cards

No need to spend lots of money buying holiday cards. Card stock paper and holiday themed duct tape are all you need to create your own quick, easy, and unique holiday cards.

What You Need:

✓ Card stock paper
✓ Holiday-themed duct tape

1 Fold card stock into cards.

2 Decorate cards with holiday themed duct tape.

TACKY TIP: Don't stop here—use the same duct tape to decorate your envelopes as well!

FUN FACT!

One of the most famous uses for duct tape was by NASA during the Apollo 13 mission. Duct tape was used to help seal a repair on the ship. Since then, astronauts won't leave Earth without it!

TACKY TIP TWO: Why wait for the holidays? Use the same steps to make note cards or thank you cards anytime during the year. Just change the paper colors and duct tape patterns to match your personality!

PARTY!!

Your next birthday party will be the talk of the town when you make all your decorations with duct tape. Go one step further and make duct tape the theme!

✔ Mark the spot with a colorful banner (see page 36).

✔ Embellish the plates.

✔ Add zip to the cups.

✔ Wrap your straws with flair.

✔ Make mini flags for your cupcakes.

✔ Bows (page 17) come in handy to decorate chairs.

✔ Add panache to your party bags.

64

✔ Who needs candy cups when you have rolls of duct tape? Or for a really creative party favor, fill a roll of duct tape with candy and wrap with cellophane. Secure with (what else?) a piece of duct tape!

✔ Personalize your water bottles.

✔ Decorate a bucket or basket to hold treats.

Here are a few more ideas:

✔ Decorate index cards for quick place holders.

✔ Long double-sided strips can be used for streamers.

✔ Double-sided strips make great napkin rings.

✔ Tape long strips directly down on your paper table cloth as a table runner.

✔ Got a big crowd? Use pieces of duct tape instead of name tags.

Quick Costumes

Stick Man

Need a 3-minute costume for Halloween? We've never made one that was easier! Turn yourself into a stick figure with the help of duct tape.

What You Need:

✓ Long-sleeved shirt and matching color pants

✓ Duct tape in a color that contrasts with the clothing

✓ Craft knife or scissors

✓ Cutting mat (if using craft knife)

1 Attach a strip of tape from the top center of the shirt to the bottom of the shirt. Note: Depending on your size, you may need to cut the tape into narrow strips.

2 Attach two strips for the shoulders starting from the center body strip extending out to the left and right.

3 Attach a strip of tape down each sleeve.

4 Create hips by attaching two short strips, at a 45-degree angle from the bottom of the body strip.

5 From the ends of the hip strips, run a strip down each leg of the pants.

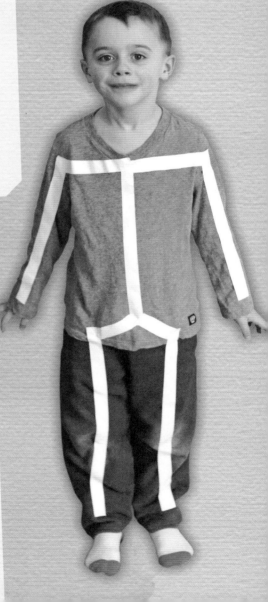

TACKY TIP: It may be easiest to get a friend to help you put the tape strips on while you are wearing the clothes.

TACKY TIP TWO: To add a little more to this costume, you can create a quick stick man mask using a paper plate and a marker!

What You Need:

✓ Black long-sleeved shirt

✓ Black pants

✓ White or glow-in-the-dark duct tape

✓ Craft knife or scissors

✓ Cutting mat (if using craft knife)

Skeleton

Make no bones about it—this costume is sure to bring smiles to trick-or-treaters of all ages! We've used white, but you could also use glow-in-the-dark duct tape for this fun costume!

1 Cut duct tape into strips and stick to the shirt as ribs. Run a long narrow strip down the center of the shirt separating the ribs. Note: Depending on your size, you may need to cut the tape into narrow strips.

2 Cut thin strips and stick to the shirt and pants for arms, shoulder blades, and legs.

3 Cut long triangles for the hipbones.

FUN FACT!

Think you have mastered these quick costumes and are ready for the big leagues? Well, have we got the contest for you! Every year, Duck® brand duct tape holds a competition in which high school students create prom dresses out of, yes, duct tape. The winner receives a $5,000 college scholarship!

Bee

One of the easiest costumes to throw together at the last minute is this adorable bumblebee. All you really need is some black clothing and yellow duct tape! You can add duct tape antennae if you want. And if you're really feeling ambitious, fashion some wings from wire coat hangers and netting!

What You Need:

✓ Black shirt and pants
✓ Yellow duct tape
✓ Scissors
✓ Duct tape antennae (optional)

1 Attach stripes of yellow duct tape to the black shirt.

2 See below for instructions on making the antennae.

Bzzzzzzzz!

Antennae

Making a pair of antennae is easy and it can be used for a variety of costumes. How about an alien? Or a robot? Or a flying insect, like a bee or a ladybug! Feel free to change the colors to suit your costume.

What You Need:

✓ 2 silver pipe cleaners
✓ Silver duct tape
✓ 2 small Styrofoam™ balls
✓ Headband
✓ Scissors

1 Insert pipe cleaners into the Styrofoam™ balls.

2 Cover the balls with silver duct tape.

3 Wrap the other end of the pipe cleaners around the top of the headband.

4 Cover the entire headband with silver duct tape.

68

What You Need:

✓ Thin cardboard

✓ Duct tape: gold, white, pink, silver

✓ 12-inch wooden dowel

✓ Craft jewels

✓ White craft glue

✓ 24 x 48-inch piece of pink tulle

✓ Craft knife

✓ Cutting mat

✓ Scissors

Princess

If you're looking for a last minute costume, turn yourself into a princess using just a few simple items (and some duct tape, of course!).

TO MAKE THE HAT:

1 Make a double-sided sheet (see page 7) from gold duct tape, large enough to roll it into a cone shape around your head. HINT: Use a piece of paper to create a cone to figure out what size sheet you will need.

2 Roll the sheet into a cone, making sure it fits comfortably on your head. Secure the cone with a couple pieces of gold tape.

3 Tuck the tulle into the top of the hat and tape in place.

The royal coach awaits!

TO MAKE THE WAND:

1 Cut a star from cardboard and cover in gold duct tape.

2 Cover dowel with white duct tape.

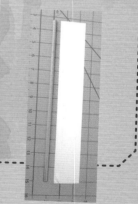

3 Make skinny strips out of pink, white, and silver duct tape. Tape them to the top of the dowel. Then tape the dowel to the back of the gold star.

4 Attach jewels to the front of the star using white craft glue.

TACKY TIP: Add some wings and your princess becomes a fairy!

Pirate

Ahoy, Matey! Avast ye lads and lassies as we're about to show ye how to easily turn some cardboard and a t-shirt into a pirate costume. Yo ho ho and a roll of duct tape!

What You Need:

✓ White t-shirt
✓ Red bandana
✓ Black yarn
✓ Cardboard or foam core board
✓ Duct tape: silver, black, and red
✓ Scissors
✓ Craft knife
✓ Cutting mat

1 Cut a sword shape from cardboard and cover it with silver duct tape.

2 Cut a handle (shaped like a "T") from cardboard and cover it with black duct tape.

3 Attach the handle to the blade using duct tape.

4 Make a 4-inch double-sided sheet with black duct tape (see page 7).

5 Cut the double-sided sheet into a patch. Use another small piece of black tape to add a length of yarn long enough to go around your head.

6 Cover a white shirt with red duct tape stripes. Add some black pants.

7 Tie a bandana around your head.

8 Add the eye patch.

Grab your sword and let the swashbuckling begin!

Bull's-eye and Arrow

You'll be the "hit" of the party with this hilarious costume!

What You Need:

✓ Duct tape: white, black, blue, red, yellow, and silver

✓ Black shirt and pants

✓ 2 pipe cleaners

✓ 2 drinking straws

✓ Headband

✓ Small piece of cardboard

✓ Scissors

✓ Cutting mat

✓ Craft knife

TO MAKE THE BULL'S-EYE:

1 Make single-sided sheets (see page 7) out of the white, black, blue, red, and yellow duct tape. The white sheet should be the biggest, and each one should be a little smaller.

2 Cut each sheet into a circle.

3 Stick the large white circle onto the center of black shirt.

4 Stick the black circle onto the white circle and so on, until you have created a bull's-eye target.

TO MAKE THE ARROW:

1 Cut a small triangle from the cardboard.

2 Cover the triangle with silver duct tape.

3 Cut two more triangles to form the tail of the arrow. Cover the tail pieces in yellow duct tape and cut small slits in the edges to look like a feather.

4 Wrap a pipe cleaner around each side of the headband. One pipe cleaner should be longer than the other.

5 Slide a drinking straw over each pipe cleaner, trimming the straws where needed. This will give the arrow some stability.

6 Cover each straw/pipe cleaner with black duct tape and attach the tail and arrowhead with tape as well.

Amanda Formaro is a Midwest mother of four who has been creating crafts for kids for over 20 years. She has been published in several major magazines including *Parents*, *Redbook*, and *Family Fun*, and websites including Disney's Family.com and spoonful.com. Her passion for crafting resonates in her blog, **CraftsbyAmanda.com**, where she shares tutorials with step-by-step photos for adults and kids alike. Amanda loves the creative process and trying new things, and especially likes making something from nothing.